AMERICAN DOCUMENTS

The Constitution

James Madison

Paul Finkelman

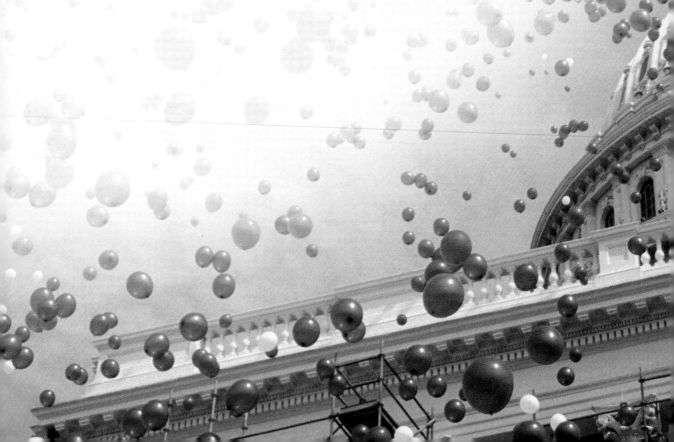

Picture Credits

Cover (flag) Photodisc/Getty Images; cover (document), 13 (bottom), 16 (bottom) courtesy Library of Congress; cover (foreground) Brand X Pictures/Getty Images; pages 1, 10, 11 (bottom), 13 (top), 15 (bottom), 16-17, 18, 20, 23 (right), 26-29 Bettmann/Corbis; pages 2-3, 4-5 Wally McNamee/Corbis; page 6 National Geographic Image Sales; page 7 Corbis; page 8 The Corcoran Gallery of Art/Corbis; page 9 (all) American Currency Exhibit/Federal Reserve Bank of San Francisco; page 11 (top) North Wind Picture Archives; page 12 Courtesy of the Architect of the Capitol; page 14 Dennis Degnan/Corbis; page 15 (top) Joseph Sohm, ChromoSohm Inc./Corbis; page 16 (top) Archivo Iconografo SA/Corbis; page 19 Hulton Archive/Getty Images; page 21 Tony Stone/Getty Images; page 22 (top) Time Life Pictures/Getty Images; page 22 (bottom) Getty Images; page 23 (left) David J. & Janice L. Frent Collection/Corbis; page 24 Eric Freeland/Corbis SABA; page 25 Reuters New Media, Inc./Corbis; page 30 Art Resource, NY.

Produced through the worldwide resources of the National Geographic Society, John M. Fahey, Jr., President and Chief Executive Officer; Gilbert M. Grosvenor, Chairman of the Board; Nina D. Hoffman, Executive Vice President and President, Books and Education Publishing Group.

Prepared by National Geographic School Publishing and Children's Books

Ericka Markman, Senior Vice President and President, Children's Books and Education Publishing Group; Steve Mico, Vice President, Editorial Director; Marianne Hiland, Executive Editor; Anita Schwartz, Project Editor; Suzanne Patrick Fonda, Children's Books Project Editor; Jim Hiscott, Design Manager; Kristin Hanneman, Illustrations Manager; Diana Bourdrez, Picture Editor; Matt Wascavage, Manager of Publishing Services; Sean Philpotts, Production Manager.

Manufacturing and Quality Management

Christopher A. Liedel, Chief Financial Officer; Phillip L. Schlosser, Director; Clifton M. Brown, Manager.

Art Direction

Dan Banks, Project Design Company

Consultants/Reviewers

Dr. Margit E. McGuire, School of Education, Seattle University, Seattle, Washington

Book Development

Nieman Inc.

Book Design

Steven Curtis Design, Inc.

Photo Research

Corrine L. Brock, In the Lupe, Inc.

ISBN: 0-7922-7937-9 (hardcover)
ISBN: 0-7922-7975-1 (library)

Library of Congress CIP data available on request

Previously published as *Documents of Freedom: The Constitution* (National Geographic Reading Expeditions), copyright © 2004
ISBN: 0-7922-4555-5 (paperback)

Published by the National Geographic Society
1145 17th Street, N.W.
Washington, D.C. 20036-4688

Printed in the U.S.A.

Table of Contents

Introduction

The Constitution is at work when a President makes the annual State of the Union Address to the three branches of government.

What would it be like if our government had no president or any one leader? What if the government could not collect taxes to pay its bills? What if each state had its own kind of money? You would have to change your Pennsylvania money into Virginia money as you traveled south. What if a criminal only had to slip out of state to escape justice? That is what the United States was like before the Constitution was written.

A new nation needs a written plan of government. When the United States declared its independence from Britain, it needed a new government. Its first plan created a weak national government that did not work well. So, Americans wrote a second plan, the U.S. Constitution. This new plan worked, and it has become a model for governments around the world! What does the U.S. Constitution say and what does it mean in our lives? Let's find out.

On Display

The original Constitution was written in 1787 on four sheets of parchment, a heavy kind of paper. It was kept in various cities until 1952, when it was placed in the National Archives Building in Washington, D.C. In 2003, a major renovation of the National Archives was completed. The entire Constitution is now on display.

First of Its Kind

The U.S. Constitution has about 4,500 words. It is the oldest and the shortest written constitution of any government in the world today.

Who Signed It?

Thirty-nine men signed the Constitution. The oldest was 81-year-old Benjamin Franklin of Pennsylvania. The youngest was Jonathan Dayton of New Jersey, who was 26.

The Clerk's Fee

The clerk who wrote out the Constitution was paid $30 for the job. That is worth about $575 today.

Visitors view the Constitution at the National Archives in Washington, D.C.

We the people of the United States, in order to form a more perfect Union... do ordain and establish this Constitution of the United States of America.

We the People

of the United States, in order to form a more perfect Union, establish Justice, insure domestic Tranquility, provide for the common defence, promote the general Welfare, and secure the Blessings of Liberty to ourselves and our Posterity, do ordain and establish this Constitution for the United States of America.

Article. I.

Article. II.

Article. III.

Article. IV.

Article V.

Article VI.

Article VII.

done

in Convention by the Unanimous Consent of the States present the Seventeenth Day of September in the Year of our Lord one thousand seven hundred and Eighty seven and of the Independance of the United States of America the Twelfth. In Witness whereof We have hereunto subscribed our Names.

First Government

By 1783, the American Revolution was over. The United States had won. However, our new national government was dangerously weak.

★

Too Little Power

George Washington kept American army officers from rebelling against the Confederation government.

This national government had been set up during the Revolution. It was based on a plan called the **Articles of Confederation**. The Confederation was a loose union of the 13 states. In this plan, the national government was weak. The state governments held most of the power. The states wanted it that way. They had just fought a war with Great Britain to escape from a strong central government.

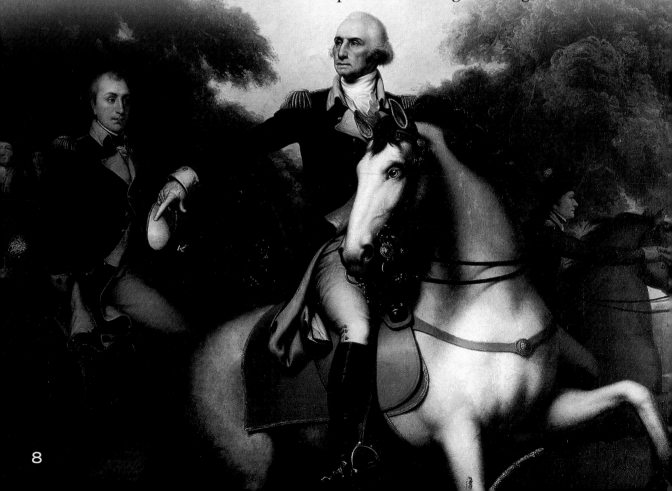

The Confederation government had so little power it could not do many of the basic things a government needs to do. The Confederation government was run by a Congress. However, there was no president to carry out the laws passed by this Congress. There were no courts to settle disagreements between citizens or between the states. Congress could not collect taxes and had no money to pay its debts.

An example of this weakness occurred near the end of the Revolution. A group of army officers was angry because Congress had not paid them or their soldiers. They were ready to march on the government and take it over. George Washington, commander of the American army, stopped them with a speech in which he appealed to their love of their country.

The 13 states ignored many of the laws the Confederation government passed. There were also conflicts between states. Some states charged taxes on things for sale from other states, just as if they were imported from foreign countries. Each state had its own form of money. Almost no one wanted to take the "continental dollars" printed by the national government. So, farmers did not know what they could get for their crops. People with goods to sell did not know what kind of money to accept. Trade between people in different states was complicated and difficult.

During the Confederation government, each state printed its own money.

Shays's rebels
took over
courthouses.

Shays's Rebellion

One event made the problem clear. It is called Shays's
Rebellion. In western Massachusetts, many farmers were not
making enough money to pay their debts or their taxes. The
people a farmer owed money to would take him to court.
The court would rule that he had to give up his land, his
farm, and his livestock to pay his debts.

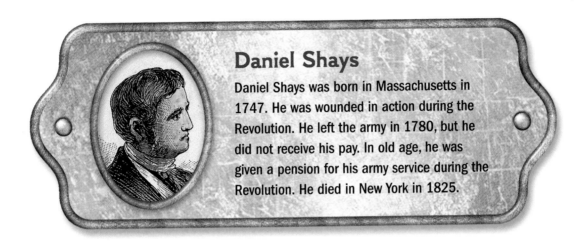

Daniel Shays

Daniel Shays was born in Massachusetts in 1747. He was wounded in action during the Revolution. He left the army in 1780, but he did not receive his pay. In old age, he was given a pension for his army service during the Revolution. He died in New York in 1825.

Many farmers lost their land. A former captain in the American army named Daniel Shays had a plan. Shays was neither a violent man nor a lawbreaker, but he felt he had to help. In August 1786, Shays led his neighbors in an armed march to close the local courts.

Tempers flared, fights broke out, and four men were killed during Shays's Rebellion.

This event terrified people. Could a group of angry farmers overturn law and order? Massachusetts authorities asked the national government to send troops to end the rebellion. There was no money to pay the soldiers. In the end, private businessmen gave $20,000 to pay the men in the state militia. Then, the militia marched out and defeated Shays's men. Shays was captured and sentenced to be hanged, but the governor of Massachusetts pardoned him.

Shays's Rebellion showed people how weak the national government was. It is a bad sign when people take the law into their own hands, like Shays and his men had done. Americans were afraid. The fate of the nation seemed to be in doubt.

Getting a Constitution

In 1786, a group of political leaders asked that all 13 states send delegates to a convention to fix the Articles of Confederation.

★

A Meeting in Philadelphia

The delegates gathered in Philadelphia, the nation's largest city. They met in the Pennsylvania State House (now called Independence Hall), where the Declaration of Independence had been signed in 1776. In February 1787, the first delegate arrived. He was James Madison of Virginia. Madison was small, soft-spoken, and looked younger than his 36 years.

(left to right)
Alexander Hamilton,
James Wilson,
James Madison,
and Benjamin
Franklin in
Franklin's garden

Madison had a keen mind and was well-prepared. He had spent the last year reading about government and history. He also had a plan, the **Virginia Plan**, for the new government. At the convention, Madison kept careful notes. Fellow delegates came to appreciate his record keeping. They gave him written copies of their speeches to put in his notes.

In early May, America's hero of the Revolution, George Washington, arrived in Philadelphia. Mounted soldiers and throngs of people came out to greet him. He went directly to the home of Benjamin Franklin. There, the two most famous men in America dined and talked over the problems of the new nation.

The other delegates were also leaders of their states and the nation. They were lawyers, landowners, and merchants. James Wilson of Pennsylvania was well-known for his knowledge of law and politics. His influence was second only to that of Madison.

One of the youngest men at the convention was handsome Alexander Hamilton of New York. He was a war hero and a brilliant lawyer. Roger Sherman of Connecticut, at 66, was one of the oldest delegates. Many delegates were slave owners, like Charles Cotesworth Pinckney of South Carolina, one of the wealthiest men in the nation. By May 28, there were 55 delegates from 11 states. New Hampshire's delegation did not arrive until mid-July. Rhode Island never sent a delegation.

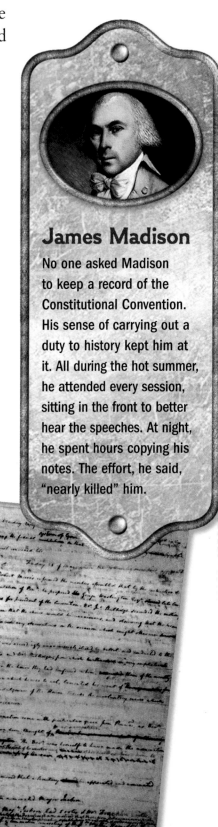

James Madison

No one asked Madison to keep a record of the Constitutional Convention. His sense of carrying out a duty to history kept him at it. All during the hot summer, he attended every session, sitting in the front to better hear the speeches. At night, he spent hours copying his notes. The effort, he said, "nearly killed" him.

Detail of page from Madison's notes at the Convention

Conflict and Compromise

As soon as the Constitutional Convention began, the delegates chose George Washington to preside. Americans trusted him, which helped to overcome fears about changing their government. The delegates also voted to keep their discussions secret. To help do this, they kept the State House doors locked. They also kept the windows closed to keep out the flies, even though it was a very hot summer in Philadelphia.

The delegates faced many problems. The most serious was how to balance power between big states and small states. Under the Articles of Confederation, each state had one vote in Congress. People from large states thought this was unfair.

The delegates met in Independence Hall, Philadelphia.

Washington's chair at the Convention had a half-sun on its back. Benjamin Franklin said he felt sure it showed a rising, not setting, sun for the United States.

Small states felt they should have as much power as big states. In Madison's Virginia Plan, states got a number of representatives in Congress based on their population. The big states wanted the Virginia Plan. The small states wanted a plan put forward by William Paterson of New Jersey. In the **New Jersey Plan**, all states got the same number of representatives.

After much debate, the delegates accepted a compromise proposed by Roger Sherman of Connecticut. Congress would have two houses, the Senate and the House of Representatives. In the Senate, each state gets two senators. In the House, representation is based on population. This agreement came to be called the **Great Compromise**.

Another important issue was how slaves should be counted. The southern states wanted to count all people. In some states, nearly half the population was enslaved. If all the slaves were counted, the South could outvote the North in the House of Representatives. Northerners did not want to count slaves at all. Slaves were property. This conflict was settled by the **Three-fifths Compromise**. The number of representatives of each state would be based on a count of all the free people plus three-fifths of the slaves.

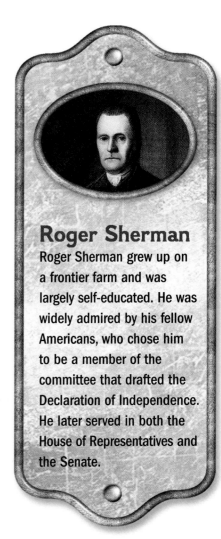

Roger Sherman
Roger Sherman grew up on a frontier farm and was largely self-educated. He was widely admired by his fellow Americans, who chose him to be a member of the committee that drafted the Declaration of Independence. He later served in both the House of Representatives and the Senate.

15

Passing the Constitution

On September 17, the Constitutional Convention finished its work. Most of the delegates signed the Constitution, but a few refused to do so. They did not like some parts of the new plan. George Mason of Virginia complained that there was no "bill of rights" guaranteeing freedom of religion, speech, and other rights. He himself had written his own state's famous Virginia Declaration of Rights.

Now that it had been written, Americans everywhere debated the new Constitution. Those who supported it were called **Federalists**. George Washington was a Federalist. So were James Madison, Alexander Hamilton, and John Jay. They wrote a series of essays, called *The Federalist,* to explain and support the Constitution. *The Federalist* persuaded many Americans that the new Constitution would provide good government.

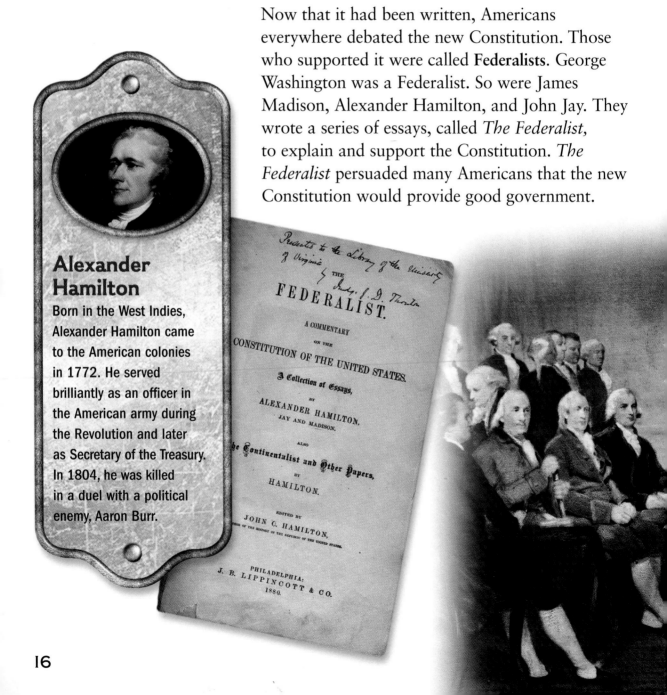

Alexander Hamilton

Born in the West Indies, Alexander Hamilton came to the American colonies in 1772. He served brilliantly as an officer in the American army during the Revolution and later as Secretary of the Treasury. In 1804, he was killed in a duel with a political enemy, Aaron Burr.

Anti-Federalists opposed the Constitution. Like George Mason, some wanted a bill of rights. Others feared the new government would be too strong. They worried that a national government, distant from their lives, would oppress them and not provide for their needs. They wanted government close to home. Former governor Patrick Henry of Virginia opposed the Constitution. He felt a strong national government would make state governments less important.

After almost a year of debate, 11 states **ratified**, or approved, the Constitution. The first to do so was tiny Delaware. The last two were Virginia and New York. In the final showdown at the Virginia ratifying convention, James Madison and his supporters defeated Patrick Henry. North Carolina and Rhode Island did not ratify the Constitution until the new government went into effect. The new Constitution was now the law of the land. To no one's surprise, George Washington was elected the first President in the new government.

The signing of the Constitution

A Closer Look

The Constitution has three parts. There is an introduction called the Preamble, seven articles that describe the plan of the national government, and the amendments, or changes to the Constitution.

★

The Preamble

The first paragraph of the Constitution states the basic purposes of the new plan of government: (1) to create a union where the states work together; (2) to create a system of laws that are fair; (3) to keep peace within the country; (4) to protect the nation from outside attack; (5) to improve the lives of all Americans; and (6) to make sure that our free society survives in the future.

New Yorkers celebrated the ratification of the Constitution in 1788.

The Articles

The seven articles set out the powers of Congress, the President, and the federal courts. The articles also explain how the states are to relate to the national government and how the Constitution can be amended, or changed. Most importantly, the articles declare that the Constitution and all laws made by Congress will be the "supreme law of the land." All states must obey the national laws and follow the Constitution.

The Amendments

The **amendments**, or changes to the Constitution, were not written at the Constitutional Convention. They were added later, when changing conditions showed a need for a change to our plan of government. Changing the Constitution is not easy. There have been only 27 amendments in more than 200 years.

"We the people"

The Constitution begins with the famous words, "We the people of the United States." This means that the government is our government. It is established by "the people," not by a king or any other authority.

"to form a more perfect Union"

The heart of the Constitution is the strengthening of the union that ties the states together.

George Washington was sworn in as the first U.S. President on April 30, 1789, at the Federal Hall in New York City.

Three Branches of Government

The Constitution created a government with three separate branches, or divisions. They are the legislative, executive, and judicial branches.

Legislative Branch

* called Congress
* includes the House of Representatives and the Senate
* makes our laws

Executive Branch

* includes the President, government agencies, and the military
* carries out our laws

Judicial Branch

* includes the Supreme Court and other federal courts
* hears cases and interprets our laws

The Legislative Branch

The Constitution begins with the Congress. The delegates started here because this branch passes the laws. It is the most important branch. It is also the part of government that is closest to the people. This branch represents the people of each state. Article 1 sets up the House of Representatives and the Senate. It says how the members of each body will be chosen, who can be a member, and how many members each body will have. The most important part of Article 1 tells what kinds of laws Congress can pass and what kinds it cannot pass. Among other things, Congress can enact taxes, borrow money, and declare war.

A serious responsibility of Congress is to declare war at the request of the President.

Congress can not favor one state over another or grant titles of nobility, such as duke or earl. Finally, Article 1 says Congress also can make any laws "necessary and proper" to carrying out its powers. This **elastic clause** was a way for future Americans to expand the meaning of the Constitution.

The Executive Branch

Article 2 describes the office of the President and who can fill the office. It also tells what powers and duties that person has. The President serves as commander-in-chief of the military. With Senate approval, the President also makes treaties and appoints ambassadors and judges. One of the President's most important duties is to give Congress "information about the State of the Union." This means the President reports on how the United States is doing and urges Congress to pass laws that the country needs.

Today, the executive branch of government is huge. It employs millions of people. The delegates never imagined how our government would grow. They gave the President enough power, however, to carry out Congress's laws. As our society grew and became more complex, so did our government.

The President leads the government from his office in the White House.

The Judicial Branch

This branch consists of the Supreme Court and other federal courts. This branch interprets the law. That means these courts hear cases to decide how the Constitution and other national laws apply to them. Article 3 creates the office of Chief Justice of the United States and tells Congress to create a Supreme Court. The Constitution also allows Congress to create other federal courts. Today, we have federal courts for trials, appeals, and special areas of the law, such as immigration. An **appeal** means a transfer of a legal case from a lower to a higher court for a new hearing.

Justices of the U.S. Supreme Court in 2003

The Supreme Court building

Checks and Balances

Government needs to have power to do its job. However, it may use this power to do wrong. Governments have used the police to take away the rights of the people. Officials have used tax money to make themselves rich. Governments have gone to war when many citizens believed it was wrong.

The delegates wanted to control the power they gave to our government. To do this, they built into the Constitution a system of **checks and balances**. They created three separate branches of government. They wanted each branch to help control the power of the others.

To take one example, Congress passes laws, but the President signs the laws. The President can **veto**, or reject, a law. However, if two-thirds of the members of the House and the Senate then vote for the law, they can override the President's veto. Later, if a legal case results from the law, the Supreme Court can decide whether the law is **unconstitutional**. In this way, all three branches of government have a role in seeing that our laws are fair.

Political cartoon attacking President Andrew Jackson for using his veto power to rule like a king

If Congress believes a President has seriously misused power, it can **impeach**, or formally charge, him or her with misconduct. The Senate puts the President on trial. If found guilty, the President can be removed from office. In U.S. history, two Presidents have been impeached and brought to trial. Neither was found guilty.

Ticket for impeachment trial of President Andrew Johnson in 1868

U.S. SENATE
Impeachment of President
ADMIT THE BEARER
APRIL 6TH 1868.

Electing the President

The Constitution gives us a way of electing the President. Did you know that a person can win the most votes in a presidential election but not become the President? This has happened in our history.

The delegates to the Constitutional Convention had many ideas about how to choose the President. They considered letting the Congress elect the President. Maybe the state legislatures would nominate the President. Some delegates thought that the people should elect the President through a **popular vote**. A popular vote is a vote of all qualified voters. Delegates from the states with small populations did not like this idea.

Voters line up to cast their ballots in New York City during the 2000 election.

In the end, the delegates decided the President would be elected by a group called the **electoral college**. The voters of each state would elect the state's "presidential electors." Each state's number of electors is its number of senators (two) plus its number of representatives in the House. The electors would meet and vote.

Today, voters mark their ballots for one of the candidates for President. States have their own rules about how to choose the electors. The Constitution shows how many electors each state gets. The electors in a state vote the way the people in their state decided, even though they do not all have to by law. Because the number of electors is not exactly like the actual number of people voting, a person can win the popular vote but lose the vote in the electoral college!

In 2000, George W. Bush was elected President by the electoral college even though he lost the popular vote.

4 The Amendments

The delegates in Philadelphia knew that they were not perfect. They understood that the Constitution might have to be changed.

★

Americans celebrate the passage of the 13th Amendment, which ended slavery, in 1865.

The delegates wanted the Constitution changed only when it was very important and when most of the people in the country agreed. So, they made changing the Constitution a difficult process. Two-thirds of each house of Congress must vote for an amendment. After that, three-quarters of the states must ratify the amendment. Only then does the amendment become part of the Constitution.

The Bill of Rights

At first, the Constitution did not include a bill of rights. Many people thought it was a mistake that the Constitution did not have one. That problem was fixed by the first ten amendments, our **Bill of Rights**. The amendments of the Bill of Rights protect the basic freedoms of individuals. These include freedom of religion, freedom of speech, freedom to protest government actions peacefully, and the right to a fair trial.

These amendments guarantee that people accused of crimes will have a lawyer. They are guaranteed that they will be given a trial held in the open—not in secret. People convicted of a crime are guaranteed they will not receive "cruel and unusual punishment." These amendments also guarantee a free government and an open society. Sometimes we may have to listen to people whose ideas we do not share. This is part of living in a free country. Freedom, as protected by the Bill of Rights, means we must tolerate those who disagree with us. It also means we respect those who have a different religion from ours or no religion at all.

The Bill of Rights guarantees freedom of expression, including disrespect to the flag. Only a Constitutional amendment could ban such disrespect.

Later Changes

After the Bill of Rights was ratified, the Constitution was
still not perfect. So, we have added another 17 amendments
since 1791. Some amendments were needed to fix things
that did not work well. Here is an example. At first, a new
President was elected in November, but did not take office
until March. This made sense in an age of horses and sailing
ships. It took time to get the news from one place to the
other. It took time for people to get to the national capital.
Now, in an age of trains, cars, and planes, this no longer
makes sense. In 1933, the 20th Amendment changed the
date the new President takes office to January 20.

Some of the most important amendments have created more freedom, liberty, and political opportunity for all Americans. The Constitution could not solve the problem of slavery. In the end, a very bloody Civil War was needed to end slavery. After the war, we added the 13th, 14th, and 15th amendments to end all slavery and make the former slaves full citizens of the United States.

Other amendments have expanded American democracy. The 15th Amendment allowed all adult men, including former slaves, to vote. The 19th Amendment allowed women to vote. The 24th Amendment says states cannot discriminate against poor people by making people pay a tax if they want to vote. The 26th Amendment allowed 18-year-olds to vote.

Decorations at Independence Hall celebrating the 200th anniversary of the signing of the Constitution

200 Years Old—and Still Working

Our Constitution has been in operation for more than 200 years. It is the oldest working constitution in the world. It is not perfect. We have changed it 27 times. Yet, for all its faults and problems, it has brought more liberty to more people than any other system of government in the history of the world. Over the years, millions of immigrants have come to the United States. One reason they came was because they understood that this nation had a strong Constitution. It guaranteed them a voice to say what they want, and the right to vote for their leaders.

The delegates in Philadelphia said in the Preamble that they wanted to create "a more perfect Union." They wanted to "establish Justice" and "secure the Blessings of Liberty" to the American people. They succeeded remarkably well.

This 1987 work by American sculptor Mike Wilkins uses license plates to celebrate the U.S. Constitution on its 200th birthday. What do the words on the plates spell out?

Glossary

amendment a change to the Constitution

Anti-Federalist a person who thought the U.S. Constitution made the national government too strong

appeal a transfer of a legal case from a lower to a higher court for a new hearing

Articles of Confederation the first plan of government for the United States

Bill of Rights the first ten amendments to the Constitution

checks and balances the system by which each branch of our government helps control the power of the others

elastic clause the part of the Constitution that permits Congress to make any laws "necessary and proper" to carrying out its powers

electoral college a group of electors chosen by the voters of each state to formally cast the state's electoral votes for President and Vice President

Federalist a supporter of the U.S. Constitution

Great Compromise the agreement by which Congress would have two houses, the Senate (where each state gets equal representation— two senators) and the House of Representatives (where representation is based on population)

impeach to formally charge a President with misconduct

New Jersey Plan New Jersey delegate William Paterson's plan of government, in which states got an equal number of representatives in Congress

popular vote a vote of all qualified voters

ratify to approve a law or official appointment

Three-fifths Compromise the agreement by which the number of each state's representatives in Congress would be based on a count of all the free people plus three-fifths of the slaves

unconstitutional going against the Constitution

veto to reject a law

Virginia Plan Virginia delegate James Madison's plan of government, in which states got a number of representatives in Congress based on their population

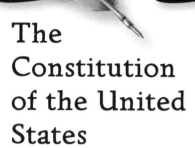

The Constitution of the United States

Preamble:

We, the People of the United States, in Order to form a more perfect Union, establish Justice, insure domestic Tranquility, provide for the common defense, promote the general Welfare, and secure the Blessings of Liberty to ourselves and our Posterity, do ordain and establish this Constitution for the United States of America.

Article I

Section 1. All legislative Powers herein granted shall be vested in a Congress of the United States, which shall consist of a Senate and House of Representatives.

Section 2. The House of Representatives shall be composed of Members chosen every second Year by the People of the several States, and the Electors in each State shall have the Qualifications requisite for Electors of the most numerous Branch of the State Legislature.

No person shall be a Representative who shall not have attained to the Age of twenty-five Years, and been seven Years a Citizen of the United States, and who shall not, when elected, be an Inhabitant of that State in which he shall be chosen.

(Representatives and direct taxes shall be apportioned among the several States which may be included within this Union, according to their respective Numbers, which shall be determined by adding to the whole Number of free Persons, including those bound to Service for a Term of Years, and excluding Indians not taxed, three-fifths of all other persons.)* The actual Enumeration shall be made within three Years after the first Meeting of the Congress of the United States, and within every subsequent

Term of ten Years, in such Manner as they shall by Law direct. The Number of Representatives shall not exceed one for every thirty Thousand, but each State shall have at Least one Representative; and until such enumeration shall be made, the State of New Hampshire shall be entitled to chuse three, Massachusetts eight, Rhode-Island and Providence Plantations one, Connecticut five, New-York six, New Jersey four, Pennsylvania eight, Delaware one, Maryland six, Virginia ten, North Carolina five, South Carolina five, and Georgia three.

When vacancies happen in the Representation from any State, the Executive Authority thereof shall issue Writs of Election to fill such Vacancies.

The House of Representatives shall chuse their Speaker and other Officers; and shall have the sole Power of Impeachment.

Section 3. The Senate of the United States shall be composed of two Senators from each State, (chosen by the Legislature thereof) for six Years; and each Senator shall have one Vote.

Immediately after they shall be assembled in Consequence of the first Election, they shall be divided as equally as may be into three Classes. The Seats of the Senators of the first Class shall be vacated at the Expiration of the second Year, of the second Class at the Expiration of the fourth Year, and of the third Class at the Expiration of the sixth Year, so that one third may be chosen every second Year; (and if vacancies happen by Resignation, or otherwise, during the Recess of the Legislature of any State, the Executive thereof may make temporary Appointments until the next Meeting of the Legislature, which shall then fill such Vacancies.)

No person shall be a Senator who shall not have attained to the Age of thirty Years, and been nine Years a Citizen of the United States, and who shall not, when elected, be an Inhabitant of that State for which he shall be chosen.

The Vice President of the United States shall be President of the Senate, but shall have no Vote, unless they be equally divided.

The Senate shall chuse their other Officers, and also a President pro tempore, in the absence of the Vice President, or when he shall exercise the Office of President of the United States.

The Senate shall have the sole Power to try all Impeachments. When sitting for that Purpose, they shall be on Oath or Affirmation. When the President of the United States is tried, the Chief Justice shall preside: And no Person shall be convicted without the Concurrence of two thirds of the Members present.

Judgment in Cases of Impeachment shall not extend further than to removal from Office, and disqualification to hold and enjoy any Office of honor, Trust or Profit under the United States: but the Party convicted shall nevertheless be liable and subject to Indictment, Trial, Judgment and Punishment, according to Law.

Section 4. The Times, Places and Manner of holding Elections for Senators and Representatives, shall be prescribed in each State by the Legislature thereof; but the Congress may at any time by Law make or alter such Regulations, except as to the Place of Chusing Senators.

The Congress shall assemble at least once in every Year, and such Meeting shall (be on the first Monday in December,) unless they shall by Law appoint a different Day.

Section 5. Each House shall be the Judge of the Elections, Returns and Qualifications of its own Members, and a Majority of each shall constitute a Quorum to do Business; but a smaller number may adjourn from day to day, and may be authorized to compel the Attendance of absent Members, in such manner, and under such Penalties as each House may provide.

Each House may determine the Rules of its Proceedings, punish its members for disorderly Behavior, and, with the Concurrence of two thirds, expel a Member.

Each House shall keep a Journal of its Proceedings, and from time to time publish the same, excepting such Parts as may in their Judgment require Secrecy; and the Yeas and Nays of the Members of either House on any question shall, at the Desire of one fifth of those Present, be entered on the Journal.

Neither House, during the Session of Congress, shall, without the Consent of the other, adjourn for more than three days, nor to any other Place than that in which the two Houses shall be sitting.

Section 6. The Senators and Representatives shall receive a Compensation for their Services, to be ascertained by Law, and paid out of the Treasury of the United States. They shall in all Cases, except Treason, Felony and Breach of the Peace, be privileged from Arrest during their Attendance at the Session of their respective Houses, and in going to and returning from the same; and for any Speech or Debate in either House, they shall not be questioned in any other Place.

No Senator or Representative shall, during the Time for which he was elected, be appointed to any civil Office under the Authority of the United States, which shall have been created, or the Emoluments whereof shall have been increased during such time; and no Person holding any Office under the United States, shall be a Member of either House during his Continuance in office.

Section 7. All bills for raising Revenue shall originate in the House of Representatives; but the Senate may propose or concur with Amendments as on other Bills.

Every Bill which shall have passed the House of Representatives and the Senate, shall, before it become a Law, be presented to the President of the United States; If he approve he shall sign it, but if not he shall return it, with his Objections to that House in which it shall have originated, who shall enter the Objections at large on their Journal, and proceed to reconsider it. If after such Reconsideration two thirds of that House shall agree to pass the Bill, it shall be sent, together with the Objections, to the other House, by which it shall likewise be reconsidered, and if approved by two thirds of that House, it shall become a Law. But in all such Cases the Votes of both Houses shall be determined by Yeas and Nays, and the names of the Persons voting for and against the Bill shall be entered on the Journal of each House respectively. If any Bill shall not be returned by the President within ten days (Sundays excepted) after it shall have been presented to him, the Same shall be a Law, in like manner as if he had signed it, unless the Congress by their Adjournment prevent its Return, in which Case it shall not be a Law.

Every order, Resolution, or Vote to which the Concurrence of the Senate and House of Representatives may be necessary (except on a question of Adjournment) shall be presented to the President of the United States; and before the Same shall take Effect, shall be approved by him, or being disapproved by him, shall be repassed by two thirds of the Senate and House of Representatives, according to the Rules and Limitations prescribed in the Case of a Bill.

Section 8. The Congress shall have Power To lay and collect Taxes, Duties, Imposts and Excises, to pay the Debts and provide for the common Defense and general Welfare of the United States; but all Duties, Imposts and Excises shall be uniform throughout the United States;

To borrow money on the credit of the United States;

To regulate Commerce with foreign Nations, and among the several States, and with the Indian Tribes;

To establish a uniform Rule of Naturalization, and uniform Laws on the subject of Bankruptcies throughout the United States;

To coin Money, regulate the Value thereof, and of foreign Coin, and fix the Standard of Weights and Measures;

To provide for the Punishment of counterfeiting the Securities and current Coin of the United States;

To establish Post Offices and post Roads;

To promote the Progress of Science and useful Arts, by securing for limited Times to Authors and Inventors the exclusive Right to their respective Writings and Discoveries;

To constitute Tribunals inferior to the Supreme Court;

To define and punish Piracies and Felonies committed on the high seas, and Offenses against the Law of Nations;

To declare War, grant Letters of Marque and Reprisal, and make Rules concerning Captures on Land and Water;

To raise and support Armies, but no Appropriation of Money to that Use shall be for a longer Term than two Years;

To provide and maintain a Navy;

To make Rules for the Government and Regulation of the land and naval Forces;

To provide for calling forth the Militia to execute the Laws of the Union, suppress Insurrections and repel Invasions;

To provide for organizing, arming, and disciplining the militia, and for governing such Part of them as may be employed in the Service of the United States, reserving to the States respectively, the Appointment of the Officers, and the Authority of training the Militia according to the discipline prescribed by Congress;

To exercise exclusive Legislation in all Cases whatsoever, over such District (not exceeding ten Miles square) as may, by Cession of particular States, and the acceptance of Congress, become the Seat of the Government of the United States, and to exercise like Authority over all Places purchased by the Consent of the Legislature of the State in which the Same shall be, for the Erection of Forts, Magazines, Arsenals, dock Yards, and other needful buildings;—And

To make all Laws which shall be necessary and proper for carrying into Execution the foregoing Powers, and all other Powers vested by this Constitution in the Government of the United States, or in any Department or Officer thereof.

Section 9. The migration or Importation of such Persons as any of the States now existing shall think proper to admit, shall not be prohibited by the Congress prior to the Year one thousand eight hundred and eight, but a tax or duty may be imposed on such Importation, not exceeding ten dollars for each Person.

The privilege of the Writ of Habeas Corpus shall not be suspended, unless when in Cases of Rebellion or Invasion the public Safety may require it.

No Bill of Attainder or ex post facto Law shall be passed.

No capitation, or other direct, Tax shall be laid, unless in Proportion to the Census or Enumeration herein before directed to be taken.

No Tax or Duty shall be laid on Articles exported from any State.

No Preference shall be given by any Regulation of Commerce or Revenue to the Ports of one State over those of another: nor shall Vessels bound to, or from, one State, be obliged to enter, clear, or pay Duties in another.

No Money shall be drawn from the Treasury, but in Consequence of Appropriations made by Law; and a regular Statement and Account of the Receipts and Expenditures of all public Money shall be published from time to time.

No Title of nobility shall be granted by the United States: and no Person holding any Office of Profit or Trust under them, shall, without the Consent of the Congress, accept of any present, Emolument, Office, or Title, of any kind whatever, from any King, Prince, or foreign State.

Section 10. No State shall enter into any Treaty, Alliance, or Confederation; grant Letters of Marque and Reprisal; coin Money; emit Bills of Credit; make Anything but gold and silver Coin a Tender in Payment of Debts; pass any Bill of Attainder, ex post facto Law,

or Law impairing the Obligation of Contracts, or grant any Title of Nobility.

No State shall, without the Consent of the Congress, lay any Imposts or Duties on Imports or Exports, except what may be absolutely necessary for executing its inspection Laws: and the net Produce of all Duties and Imposts, laid by any State on Imports or Exports, shall be for the Use of the Treasury of the United States; and all such Laws shall be subject to the Revision and Control of the Congress.

No State shall, without the Consent of Congress, lay any duty of Tonnage, keep Troops, or Ships of War in time of Peace, enter into any Agreement or Compact with another State, or with a foreign Power, or engage in War, unless actually invaded, or in such imminent Danger as will not admit of delay.

Article II

Section 1. The executive Power shall be vested in a President of the United States of America. He shall hold his Office during the Term of four Years, and, together with the Vice President, chosen for the same Term, be elected, as follows.

Each State shall appoint, in such Manner as the Legislature thereof may direct, a Number of Electors, equal to the whole Number of Senators and Representatives to which the State may be entitled in the Congress: but no Senator or Representative, or Person holding an Office of Trust or Profit under the United States, shall be appointed an Elector.

(The Electors shall meet in their respective States, and vote by Ballot for two persons, of whom one at least shall not be an Inhabitant of the same State with themselves. And they shall make a List of all the Persons voted for, and of the Number of Votes for each; which List they shall sign and certify, and transmit sealed to the Seat of the Government of the United States, directed to the President of the Senate. The President of the Senate shall, in the Presence of the Senate and House of Representatives, open all the Certificates, and the Votes shall then be counted. The Person having the greatest Number of Votes shall be the President, if such Number be a Majority of the whole Number of Electors appointed; and if there be more than one who have such Majority, and have an equal Number of Votes, then the House of Representatives shall immediately chuse by Ballot one of them for President; and if no Person have a Majority, then from the five highest on the List the said House shall in like Manner chuse the President. But in chusing the President, the Votes shall be taken by States, the representation from each State having one Vote; A quorum for this Purpose shall consist of a Member or Members from two thirds of the States, and a Majority of all the States shall be necessary to a Choice. In every Case, after the Choice of the President, the Person having the greatest Number of Votes of the Electors shall be the Vice President. But if there should remain two or more who have equal Votes, the Senate shall chuse from them by Ballot the Vice-President.)

The Congress may determine the Time of chusing the Electors, and the Day on which they shall give their Votes; which Day shall be the same throughout the United States.

No person except a natural born Citizen, or a Citizen of the United States, at the time of the Adoption of this Constitution, shall be eligible to the Office of President; neither shall any Person be eligible to that Office who shall not have attained to the Age of thirty five Years, and been fourteen Years a Resident within the United States.

In Case of the Removal of the President from Office, or of his Death, Resignation, or Inability to discharge the Powers and Duties of the said Office, the same shall devolve on the Vice President, and the Congress may by Law provide for the Case of Removal, Death, Resignation or Inability, both of the President and Vice President, declaring what Officer shall then act as President, and such Officer shall act accordingly, until the Disability be removed, or a President shall be elected.

The President shall, at stated Times, receive for his Services, a Compensation, which shall neither be encreased nor diminished during the Period for which he shall have been elected, and he shall not receive within that Period any other Emolument from the United States, or any of them.

Before he enter on the Execution of his Office, he shall take the following Oath or Affirmation:— "I do solemnly swear (or affirm) that I will faithfully execute the Office of President of the United States, and will to the best of my Ability, preserve, protect and defend the Constitution of the United States."

Section 2. The President shall be Commander in Chief of the Army and Navy of the United States, and of the Militia of the several States, when called into the actual Service of the United States; he may require the Opinion, in writing, of the principal Officer in each of the executive Departments, upon any subject relating to the Duties of their respective Offices, and he shall have Power to Grant Reprieves and Pardons for Offenses against the United States, except in Cases of Impeachment.

He shall have Power, by and with the Advice and Consent of the Senate, to make Treaties, provided two thirds of the Senators present concur; and he shall nominate, and by and with the Advice and Consent of the Senate, shall appoint Ambassadors, other public Ministers and Consuls, judges of the Supreme Court, and all other Officers of the United States, whose Appointments are not herein otherwise provided for, and which shall be established by Law: but the Congress may by Law vest the Appointment of such inferior Officers, as they think proper, in the President alone, in the Courts of Law, or in the Heads of Departments.

The President shall have Power to fill up all Vacancies that may happen during the Recess of the Senate, by granting Commissions which shall expire at the End of their next Session.

Section 3. He shall from time to time give to the Congress Information of the State of the Union, and recommend to their Consideration such Measures as he shall judge necessary and expedient; he may, on extraordinary Occasions, convene both Houses, or either of them, and in Case of Disagreement between them, with Respect to the Time of Adjournment, he may adjourn them to such Time as he shall think proper; he shall receive Ambassadors and other public Ministers; he shall take Care that the Laws be faithfully executed, and shall Commission all the Officers of the United States.

Section 4. The President, Vice President and all civil Officers of the United States, shall be removed from Office on Impeachment for, and Conviction of, Treason, Bribery, or other high Crimes and Misdemeanors.

Article III

Section 1. The judicial Power of the United States, shall be vested in one supreme Court, and in such inferior Courts as the Congress may from time to time ordain and establish. The Judges, both of the supreme and inferior Courts, shall hold their Offices during good Behaviour, and shall, at stated Times, receive for their Services, a Compensation, which shall not be diminished during their Continuance in office.

Section 2. The judicial Power shall extend to all Cases, in Law and Equity, arising under this Constitution, the Laws of the United States, and Treaties made, or which shall be made, under their Authority;—to all Cases affecting Ambassadors, other public Ministers and Consuls;—to all Cases of admiralty and maritime Jurisdiction;—to Controversies to which the United States shall be a Party;—to Controversies between two or more States;— between a State and Citizens of another State;—between Citizens of different States;— between Citizens of the same State claiming Lands under Grants of different States, and between a State, or the Citizens thereof, and foreign States, Citizens or Subjects.

In all Cases affecting Ambassadors, other public Ministers and Consuls, and those in which a State shall be Party, the supreme Court shall have original Jurisdiction. In all the other Cases before mentioned, the supreme Court shall have appellate Jurisdiction, both as to Law and Fact, with such Exceptions, and under such Regulations as the Congress shall make.

The trial of all Crimes, except in Cases of Impeachment, shall be by Jury; and such trial shall be held in the State where the said Crimes shall have been committed; but when not committed within any State, the Trial shall be at such Place or Places as the Congress may by Law have directed.

Section 3. Treason against the United States, shall consist only in levying War against them, or in adhering to their Enemies, giving them Aid and Comfort. No Person shall be convicted of Treason unless on the Testimony of two Witnesses to the same overt Act, or on Confession in open Court.

The Congress shall have Power to declare the Punishment of Treason, but no Attainder of Treason shall work Corruption of Blood, or Forfeiture except during the Life of the Person attainted.

Article IV

Section 1. Full Faith and Credit shall be given in each State to the public Acts, Records, and judicial Proceedings of every other State. And the Congress may by general Laws prescribe the Manner in which such Acts, Records, and Proceedings shall be proved, and the Effect thereof.

Section 2. The Citizens of each State shall be entitled to all Privileges and Immunities of Citizens in the several States.

A Person charged in any State with Treason, Felony, or other Crime, who shall flee from Justice, and be found in another State, shall on demand of the executive Authority of the State from which he fled, be delivered up, to be removed to the State having Jurisdiction of the Crime.

(No Person held to Service or Labor in one State, under the Laws thereof, escaping into another, shall, in Consequence of any Law or Regulation therein, be discharged from such Service or Labor, but shall be delivered up on Claim of the Party to whom such Service or Labor may be Due.)

Section 3. New States may be admitted by the Congress into this Union; but no new States shall be formed or erected within the Jurisdiction of any other State; nor any State be formed by the Junction of two or more States, or parts of States, without the Consent of the Legislatures of the States concerned as well as of the Congress.

The Congress shall have Power to dispose of and make all needful Rules and Regulations respecting the Territory or other Property belonging to the United States; and nothing in this Constitution shall be so construed as to Prejudice any Claims of the United States, or of any particular State.

Section 4. The United States shall guarantee to every State in this Union a Republican Form of Government, and shall protect each of them against Invasion; and on Application of the Legislature, or of the Executive (when the Legislature cannot be convened) against domestic Violence.

Article V

The Congress, whenever two thirds of both Houses shall deem it necessary, shall propose Amendments to this Constitution, or, on the Application of the Legislatures of two thirds of the several States, shall call a Convention for proposing Amendments, which, in either Case, shall be valid to all Intents and Purposes, as part of this Constitution, when ratified by the Legislatures of three fourths of the several States, or by Conventions in three fourths thereof, as the one or the other Mode of

Ratification may be proposed by the Congress: Provided that no Amendment which may be made prior to the Year One thousand eight hundred and eight shall in any Manner affect the first and fourth Clauses in the Ninth Section of the first Article; and that no State, without its Consent, shall be deprived of its equal Suffrage in the Senate.

Article VI

All Debts contracted and Engagements entered into, before the Adoption of this Constitution, shall be as valid against the United States under this Constitution, as under the Confederation.

This Constitution, and the Laws of the United States which shall be made in Pursuance thereof; and all Treaties made, or which shall be made, under the Authority of the United States, shall be the supreme Law of the Land; and the Judges in every State shall be bound thereby, Anything in the Constitution or Laws of any State to the Contrary notwithstanding.

The Senators and Representatives before mentioned, and the Members of the several State Legislatures, and all executive and judicial Officers, both of the United States and of the several States, shall be bound by Oath or Affirmation, to support this Constitution; but no religious Test shall ever be required as a Qualification to any Office or public Trust under the United States.

Article VII

The Ratification of the Conventions of nine States, shall be sufficient for the Establishment of this Constitution between the States so ratifying the Same.

Done in Convention by the unanimous Consent of the States present the Seventeenth Day of September in the Year of our Lord one thousand seven hundred and Eighty seven and of theIndependence of the United States of America the Twelfth.

In witness whereof We have hereunto subscribed our Names.

Amendments 1–10: The Bill of Rights
Ratified December 15, 1791

Amendment I
Congress shall make no law respecting an establishment of religion, or prohibiting the free exercise thereof; or abridging the freedom of speech, or of the press; or the right of the people peaceably to assemble, and to petition the Government for a redress of grievances.

Amendment II
A well regulated Militia, being necessary to the security of a free State, the right of the people to keep and bear Arms, shall not be infringed.

Amendment III
No Soldier shall, in time of peace be quartered in any house, without the consent of the Owner, nor in time of war, but in a manner to be prescribed by law.

Amendment IV
The right of the people to be secure in their persons, houses, papers, and effects, against unreasonable searches and seizures, shall not be violated, and no Warrants shall issue, but upon probable cause, supported by Oath or affirmation, and particularly describing the place to be searched, and the persons or things to be seized.

Amendment V

No person shall be held to answer for a capital, or otherwise infamous crime, unless on a presentment or indictment of a Grand Jury, except in cases arising in the land or naval forces, or in the Militia, when in actual service in time of War or public danger; nor shall any person be subject for the same offence to be twice put in jeopardy of life or limb; nor shall be compelled in any criminal case to be a witness against himself, nor be deprived of life, liberty, or property, without due process of law; nor shall private property be taken for public use,without just compensation.

Amendment VI

In all criminal prosecutions, the accused shall enjoy the right to a speedy and public trial, by an impartial jury of the State and district wherein the crime shall have been committed, which district shall have been previously ascertained by law, and to be informed of the nature and cause of the accusation; to be confronted with the witnesses against him; to have compulsory process for obtaining witnesses in his favor, and to have the Assistance of Counsel for his defence.

Amendment VII

In suits at common law, where the value in controversy shall exceed twenty dollars, the right of trial by jury shall be preserved, and no fact tried by a jury, shall be otherwise reexamined in any Court of the United States, than according to the rules of the common law.

Amendment VIII

Excessive bail shall not be required, nor excessive fines imposed, nor cruel and unusual punishments inflicted.

Amendment IX

The enumeration in the Constitution, of certain rights, shall not be construed to deny or disparage others retained by the people.

Amendment X

The powers not delegated to the United States by the Constitution, nor prohibited by it to the States, are reserved to the States respectively, or to the people.

Amendments 11–27

Amendment XI
*Proposed by Congress March 4, 1794;
Ratified February 7, 1795.*

Note: Article III, section 2, of the Constitution was modified by Amendment XI.

The Judicial power of the United States shall not be construed to extend to any suit in law or equity, commenced or prosecuted against one of the United States by Citizens of another State, or by Citizens or Subjects of any Foreign State.

Amendment XII
*Proposed by Congress December 9, 1803;
Ratified June 15, 1804.*

Note: A portion of Article II, section 1 of the Constitution was superseded by Amendment XII.

The Electors shall meet in their respective states and vote by ballot for President and Vice-President, one of whom, at least, shall not be an inhabitant of the same state with themselves; they shall name in their ballots the person voted for as

President, and in distinct ballots the person voted for as Vice-President, and they shall make distinct lists of all persons voted for as President, and of all persons voted for as Vice-President, and of the number of votes for each, which lists they shall sign and certify, and transmit sealed to the seat of the government of the United States, directed to the President of the Senate;—the President of the Senate shall, in presence of the Senate and House of Representatives, open all the certificates and the votes shall then be counted;—The person having the greatest number of votes for President, shall be the President, if such number be a majority of the whole number of Electors appointed; and if no person have such majority, then from the persons having the highest numbers not exceeding three on the list of those voted for as President, the House of Representatives shall choose immediately, by ballot, the President. But in choosing the President, the votes shall be taken by states, the representation from each state having one vote; a quorum for this purpose shall consist of a member or members from two-thirds of the states, and a majority of all the states shall be necessary to a choice. (And if the House of Representatives shall not choose a President whenever the right of choice shall devolve upon them, before the fourth day of March next following, then the Vice-President shall act as President, as in case of the death or other constitutional disability of the President.) *The person having the greatest number of votes as Vice-President, shall be the Vice-President, if such number be a majority of the whole number of Electors appointed, and if no person have a majority, then from the two highest numbers on the list, the Senate shall choose the Vice-President; a quorum for the purpose shall consist of two-thirds of the whole number of Senators, and a majority of the whole number shall be necessary

to a choice. But no person constitutionally ineligible to the office of President shall be eligible to that of Vice-President of the United States.

*Superseded by section 3 of Amendment XX.

Amendment XIII
Proposed by Congress January 31, 1865;
Ratified December 6, 1865.

Note: A portion of Article IV, section 2, lof the Constitution was superseded by Amendment XIII.

Section 1. Neither slavery nor involuntary servitude, except as a punishment for crime whereof the party shall have been duly convicted, shall exist within the United States, or any place subject to their jurisdiction.

Section 2. Congress shall have power to enforce this article by appropriate legislation.

Amendment XIV
Proposed by Congress June 13, 1866;
Ratified July 9, 1868.

Note: Article I, section 2, of the Constitution was modified by section 2 of Amendment XIV.

Section 1. All persons born or naturalized in the United States, and subject to the jurisdiction thereof, are citizens of the United States and of the State wherein they reside. No State shall make or enforce any law which shall abridge the privileges or immunities of citizens of the United States; nor shall any State deprive any person of life, liberty, or property, without due process of law; nor deny to any person within its jurisdiction the equal protection of the laws.

Section 2. Representatives shall be apportioned among the several States according to their respective numbers, counting the whole number of persons in each State, excluding Indians not taxed. But when the right to vote at any election for the choice of electors for President and Vice-President of the United States, Representatives in Congress, the Executive and Judicial officers of a State, or the members of the Legislature thereof, is denied to any of the male inhabitants of such State, (being twenty-one years of age,) and citizens of the United States, or in any way abridged, except for participation in rebellion, or other crime, the basis of representation therein shall be reduced in the proportion which the number of such male citizens shall bear to the whole number of male citizens twenty-one years of age in such State.

Section 3. No person shall be a Senator or Representative in Congress, or elector of President and Vice-President, or hold any office, civil or military, under the United States, or under any State, who, having previously taken an oath, as a member of Congress, or as an officer of the United States, or as a member of any State legislature, or as an executive or judicial officer of any State, to support the Constitution of the United States, shall have engaged in insurrection or rebellion against the same, or given aid or comfort to the enemies thereof. But Congress may by a vote of two-thirds of each House, remove such disability.

Section 4. The validity of the public debt of the United States, authorized by law, including debts incurred for payment of pensions and bounties for services in suppressing insurrection or rebellion, shall not be questioned. But neither the United States nor any State shall assume or pay any debt or obligation incurred in aid of insurrection or rebellion against the United States, or any claim for the loss or emancipation of any slave; but all such debts, obligations and claims shall be held illegal and void.

Section 5. The Congress shall have power to enforce, by appropriate legislation, the provisions of this article.

Amendment XV
Proposed by Congress February 26, 1869; Ratified February 3, 1870.

Section 1. The right of citizens of the United States to vote shall not be denied or abridged by the United States or by any State on account of race, color, or previous condition of servitude—

Section 2. The Congress shall have power to enforce this article by appropriate legislation.

Amendment XVI
Proposed by Congress July 12, 1909; Ratified February 3, 1913.

Note: Article I, section 9, of the Constitution was modified by Amendment XVI.

The Congress shall have power to lay and collect taxes on incomes, from whatever source derived, without apportionment among the several States, and without regard to any census or enumeration.

Amendment XVII
Proposed by Congress May 13, 1912; Ratified April 8, 1913.

Note: Article I, section 3, of the Constitution was modified by Amendment XVII.

The Senate of the United States shall be composed of two Senators from each State, elected by the people thereof, for six years; and each Senator shall have one vote. The electors in each State shall have the qualifications requisite for electors of the most numerous branch of the State legislatures.

When vacancies happen in the representation of any State in the Senate, the executive authority of such State shall issue writs of election to fill such vacancies: Provided, That the legislature of any State may empower the executive thereof to make temporary appointments until the people fill the vacancies by election as the legislature may direct.

This amendment shall not be so construed as to affect the election or term of any Senator chosen before it becomes valid as part of the Constitution.

Amendment XVIII
Proposed by Congress December 18, 1917; Ratified January 16, 1919: Repealed by Amendment XXI.

Section 1. After one year from the ratification of this article the manufacture, sale, or transportation of intoxicating liquors within, the importation thereof into, or the exportation thereof from the United States and all territory subject to the jurisdiction thereof for beverage purposes is hereby prohibited.

Section 2. The Congress and the several States shall have concurrent power to enforce this article by appropriate legislation.

Section 3. This article shall be inoperative unless it shall have been ratified as an amendment to the Constitution by the legislatures of the several States as provided in the Constitution, within seven years from the date of the submission hereof to the States by the Congress.

Amendment XIX
Proposed by Congress June 4, 1919; Ratified August 18, 1920.

The right of citizens of the United States to vote shall not be denied or abridged by the United States or by any State on account of sex.

Congress shall have power to enforce this Article by appropriate legislation.

Amendment XX
Proposed by Congress March 2, 1932; Ratified January 23, 1933.

Note: Article I, section 4, of the Constitution was modified by section 2 of this amendment. In addition, a portion of Amendment XII was superseded by section 3.

Section 1. The terms of the President and Vice President shall end at noon on the 20th day of January, and the terms of Senators and Representatives at noon on the 3rd day of

January, of the years in which such terms would have ended if this article had not been ratified; and the terms of their successors shall then begin.

Section 2. The Congress shall assemble at least once in every year, and such meeting shall begin at noon on the 3d day of January, unless they shall by law appoint a different day.

Section 3. If, at the time fixed for the beginning of the term of the President, the President elect shall have died, the Vice President elect shall become President. If a President shall not have been chosen before the time fixed for the beginning of his term, or if the President elect shall have failed to qualify, then the Vice President elect shall act as President until a President shall have qualified; and the Congress may by law provide for the case wherein neither a President elect nor a Vice President shall have qualified, declaring who shall then act as President, or the manner in which one who is to act shall be selected, and such person shall act accordingly until a President or Vice President shall have qualified.

Section 4. The Congress may by law provide for the case of the death of any of the persons from whom the House of Representatives may choose a President whenever the right of choice shall have devolved upon them, and for the case of the death of any of the persons from whom the Senate may choose a Vice President whenever the right of choice shall have devolved upon them.

Section 5. Sections 1 and 2 shall take effect on the 15th day of October following the ratification of this article.

Section 6. This article shall be inoperative unless it shall have been ratified as an amendment to the Constitution by the legislatures of three-fourths of the several States within seven years from the date of its submission.

Amendment XXI
Proposed by Congress February 20, 1933; Ratified December 5, 1933.

Section 1. The eighteenth article of amendment to the Constitution of the United States is hereby repealed.

Section 2. The transportation or importation into any State, Territory, or possession of the United States for delivery or use therein of intoxicating liquors, in violation of the laws thereof, is hereby prohibited.

Section 3. This article shall be inoperative unless it shall have been ratified as an amendment to the Constitution by conventions in the several States, as provided in the Constitution, within seven years from the date of the submission hereof to the States by the Congress.

Amendment XXII
Proposed by Congress March 24, 1947; Ratified February 27, 1951.

Section 1. No person shall be elected to the office of the President more than twice, and no person who has held the office of President, or acted as President, for more than two years of a term to which some other person was elected President shall be elected to the office of President more than once. But this Article shall not apply to any person holding the office of President when this Article was proposed by the Congress, and shall not prevent any person who may be holding the office of President, or acting as President, during the term within which this Article becomes operative from holding the office of President or acting as President during the remainder of such term.

Section 2. This article shall be inoperative unless it shall have been ratified as an amendment to the Constitution by the legislatures of three-fourths of the several States within seven years from the date of its submission to the States by the Congress.

Amendment XXIII
Proposed by Congress June 16, 1960;
Ratified March 29, 1961.

Section 1. The District constituting the seat of Government of the United States shall appoint in such manner as the Congress may direct:

A number of electors of President and Vice President equal to the whole number of Senators and Representatives in Congress to which the District would be entitled if it were a State, but in no event more than the least populous State; they shall be in addition to those appointed by the States, but they shall be considered, for the purposes of the election of President and Vice President, to be electors appointed by a State; and they shall meet in the District and perform such duties as provided by the twelfth article of amendment.

Section 2. The Congress shall have power to enforce this article by appropriate legislation.

Amendment XXIV
Proposed by Congress August 27, 1962;
Ratified January 23, 1964.

The right of citizens of the United States to vote in any primary or other election for President or Vice President, for electors for President or Vice President, or for Senator or Representative in Congress, shall not be denied or abridged by the United States or any State by reason of failure to pay any poll tax or other tax.

Section 2. The Congress shall have power to enforce this article by appropriate legislation.

Amendment XXV
Proposed by Congress July 6, 1965;
Ratified February 10, 1967.

Note: Article II, section 1, of the Constitution was affected by Amendment XXV.

Section 1. In case of the removal of the President from office or of his death or resignation, the Vice President shall become President.

Section 2. Whenever there is a vacancy in the office of the Vice President, the President shall nominate a Vice President who shall take office upon confirmation by a majority vote of both houses of Congress.

Section 3. Whenever the President transmits to the President pro tempore of the Senate and the Speaker of the House of Representatives his written declaration that he is unable to discharge the powers and duties of his office, and until he transmits to them a written declaration to the contrary, such powers and duties shall be discharged by the Vice President as Acting President.

Section 4. Whenever the Vice President and a majority of either the principal officers of the executive departments or of such other body as Congress may by law provide, transmit to the President pro tempore of the Senate and the Speaker of the House of Representatives their written declaration that the President is unable to discharge the powers and duties of his office, the Vice President shall immediately assume the powers and duties of the office as Acting President.

Thereafter, when the President transmits to the President pro tempore of the Senate and the Speaker of the House of Representatives his written declaration that no inability exists, he shall resume the powers and duties of his office unless the Vice President and a majority of either the principal officers of the executive department or of such other body as Congress may by law provide, transmit within four days to the President pro tempore of the Senate and the Speaker of the House of Representatives their written declaration that the President is unable to discharge the powers and duties of his office. Thereupon Congress shall decide the issue, assembling within forty-eight hours for that purpose if not in session. If the Congress, within twenty-one days after receipt of the latter written declaration, or, if Congress is not in session, within twenty-one days after Congress is required to assemble, determines by two-thirds vote of both Houses that the

President is unable to discharge the powers and duties of his office, the Vice President shall continue to discharge the same as Acting President; otherwise, the President shall resume the powers and duties of his office.

Amendment XXVI
*Proposed by Congress March 23, 1971;
Ratified July 1, 1971.*

Note: Amendment XIV, section 2, of the Constitution was modified by section 1 of Amendment XXVI.

Section 1. The right of citizens of the United States, who are eighteen years of age or older, to vote shall not be denied or abridged by the United States or by any State on account of age.

Section 2. The Congress shall have the power to enforce this article by appropriate legislation.

Amendment XXVII
*Proposed by Congress Sept. 25, 1789;
Ratified May 7, 1992.*

No law, varying the compensation for the services of the Senators and Representatives, shall take effect, until an election of representatives shall have intervened.

Index